Science Technology Engineering Math
STEM STARTERS FOR KIDS

W9-BMR-283

SCIENCE EXPERIMENTS AT HOME

IN THE BATHROOM pages 2 to 13

OUTDOORS pages 14 to 29

IN THE KITCHEN pages 30 to 39

IN YOUR BEDROOM pages 40 to 47

WORDS TO KNOW/ANSWERS page 48

by Susan Martineau and illustrated by Vicky Barker

© b small publishing ltd. 2018 • First Racehorse for Young Readers Edition 2018 • Production: Madeleine Ehm; Science Advisor: Kathryn Higgins; Publisher: Sam Hutchinson; Editorial: Eryl Nash. • All rights reserved. No part of this book may be reproduced in any manner without the express written consent of the publisher, except in the case of brief excepts in critical reviews or articles. • All inquiries should be addressed to Racehorse for Young Readers, 307 West 36th Street, 11th Floor, New York, NY 10018. Racehorse for Young Readers™ books may be purchased in bulk at special discounts for sales promotions, corporate gifts, fund-raising or education purposes. Special editions can also be created to specifications. For details, contact the Special Sales Department at Skyhorse Publishing, 307 West 36th Street, 11th Floor, New York, NY 10018 or info@skyhorsepublishing.com. • Racehorse for Young Readers is a pending trademark of Skyhorse Publishing, Inc.®, a Delaware corporation. • Visit our website at skyhorsepublishing.com •
10 9 8 7 6 5 4 3 • ISBN: 978-1-63158-298-1 • Printed in China

Be a Bathroom Scientist

Scientists learn about the world around us by doing experiments. You will learn about the science in your bathroom in this part of the book. You won't need any special equipment for these experiments. They use everyday things you'll probably find at home already, but don't forget to ask a grown-up before using them and, before you begin, always read through the whole experiment to make sure you have everything you need.

???
Quick Quizzer!

Answers are on page 48.

🚫 BE SAFE!
Never play with the medicines or cleaning chemicals you might have in your bathroom.

Keep a notebook handy so you can draw or write up what happens like a real scientist. You can make up your own experiments too.

Be careful when you use the hot tap to make sure the water is not too hot.

Words to Know
Special science words are explained on page 48.

Misty Mirrors

You can do this experiment the next time
you take a bath or shower.
It'll make getting clean more fun!

1. Shut the bathroom door (but don't lock it!)

2. Run a nice warm bath or shower.

3. Watch what happens to the windows and mirrors in the bathroom.

The warm bath or shower water gives off a **gas** called **water vapor**. This **water vapor** is made when the **liquid** bath or shower water is warmer than the air in the room. When the **water vapor** touches something cold, like a mirror or window, it turns back into drops of **liquid** again. This is called **condensation**.

Quick Warning!

Always be very careful when running hot water. Ask a grown-up to stand by.

Don't leave taps dripping as this wastes water.

Try This!

Breathe hard on a cold mirror and see what your warm breath does to it.

? ? ?

Quick Quizzer!

Can you think of another word for water vapor?

Bubble Fun

A bubbly bath is lovely but have you ever wondered how those soapy bubbles are made? This experiment shows you what is happening.

1. Half fill a sink with water.

2. Pour a bit of bubble bath into the water.

3. Put a straw into the water and blow!

Bathroom

6

Quick Quizzer!

What's the name of the soap we use to wash our hair?

When you blow into the water, you make loads of bubbles. The bubble bath makes the water **elastic**, or stretchy, so that it holds the air you are blowing into it. If you blow into water without the bubble bath, the water on its own cannot hold the air.

Did You Know?

Your skin never stops growing. When you wash yourself, soap loosens dirt from the skin and also washes away some dead skin. You might find that your fingertips feel smoother after washing your hands!

Always wash your hands after going to the bathroom to wash off any germs.

Float a Boat

How do boats manage to float on the top of water instead of sinking? In this experiment you are going to make one and find out. You need two balls of modeling clay.

1. Make one ball of clay into a boat shape.

2. Fill the sink with water.

3. Place the clay ball on the water.

4. Now place the clay boat on the water.

The ball of clay sinks to the bottom while the boat **floats**. The boat stays on the **surface** of the water because there is air between the sides of it. This makes it light for its size. The ball has no air inside it. It is **solid** and heavy for its size, so it sinks.

Quick Quizzer!

Do you think a toothbrush will sink or float?

Try This!

See if other things in the bathroom float or sink in the water. You could try bottles of shampoo, bars of soap or toothbrushes.

Write or draw which things sink or float in your notebook.

Beaker Magic

This is a great trick to play on your friends and family. They really won't believe it! Use a plastic beaker just in case you drop it by accident.

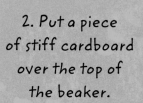

1. Half fill a plastic beaker with water.

2. Put a piece of stiff cardboard over the top of the beaker.

3. Hold the cardboard firmly in place and turn the beaker upside down.

4. Take your hand away from the cardboard.

Do this experiment over the bath or sink!

How It Works – Let's Take a Closer Look!

Air all around us is pushing up, down and sideways on everything it touches. This is called **air pressure**. The air pushes up on the cardboard too. It pushes up more strongly than the water and air inside the beaker push down. This is why the water does not fall out.

Try This!

Blow up a balloon. If you press your hand against it you can feel the air inside it pushing back.

Quick Fact

Air inside your bicycle tires pushes back too. That's why they can carry your weight as you ride along.

Bathroom

11

Toothbrush Trick

Light can play some funny tricks on our eyes. This experiment will show you a light trick with a toothbrush.

1. Half fill a clear, plastic beaker with water.

2. Put your toothbrush into the beaker.

3. Have a look at the toothbrush through the sides of the beaker.

The part of the toothbrush under the water looks bent. Light moves more slowly through water than through air. As the light slows down, it changes direction and enters your eyes from a different angle. This is why things in water look bent even though they are really straight. It is called **refraction**.

Don't forget to clean your teeth twice a day!

? ? ?
Quick Quizzer

Will the toothbrush look bent if you put it in the beaker without water?

Try This!

Next time you go swimming, stand in the pool and look down at your legs. They look short and stubby because of refraction.

Bathroom

13

Be an Outdoor Scientist

You will learn about the science in your garden or park in this section of the book. You won't need any special equipment for any of these experiments. You'll be using everyday things you probably have at home already, but remember to ask a grown-up before using them. Don't forget to read through the experiment before you start to make sure you have everything ready.

BE SAFE!

Ask a grown-up before you go out into the garden and never go to the park on your own.

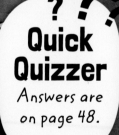

Keep a notebook handy so you can draw or write up what happens like a real scientist. You can make up your own experiments too.

Words to Know
Special science words are explained on page 48.

Wash your hands when you've finished outside.

Never eat anything you find in the garden or park. Some plants and berries can be very bad for you.

Quick Quizzer
Answers are on page 48.

Worm Home

You'll need three or four earthworms for this experiment. Look for them in freshly dug soil or under stones and logs. Pick them up very carefully so you don't hurt them. Leave the Worm Home in a cool, dark place for a few days and watch what the worms do.

1. Ask a grown-up to help cut the top off a plastic bottle.

2. Put layers of soil and sand in the bottle. Sprinkle with water.

3. Place some leaves and grass on top. Gently add your worms.

4. Tape some dark paper around the bottle. Put it in a cool, dark place.

Outdoors

The earthworms make tunnels through the soil and sand layers. In the garden these tunnels help air and water to reach the roots of plants. Worms also pull leaves down into the soil and this makes **nutrients**, or food, for plants. Worms help the plants to grow well.

Worm casts are curly piles of soil left behind by worms. It's worm poo.

Worm Warning!

Set your worms free after a few days!

Quick Quizzer!

Which garden creature loves to eat worms?

Clue: there's one on this page.

? ? ?

Did You Know?

The largest earthworms in the world live in Australia, South Africa and South America. They can be up to 3 meters long!

Bug Hunt

See what mini-beasts you can find living in your garden or in the park. The best time to look for them is in warm weather when creepy crawlies are the most active. You might want to wear gardening gloves when you are poking about looking for bugs!

1. Take a notebook, magnifying glass and pencil out into the garden or the park.

2. Choose a small area of flowerbed or lawn. Look in the soil, under stones and in long grass.

3. When you find a bug, draw it in your notebook. Count the legs, wings and parts of its body. Is it wriggling or crawling?

Beetle **? ? ?**

Butterfly

Quick Quizzer!

What has eight legs and spins a web?

Centipede

Caterpillar

The proper name for a creepy crawly is an **invertebrate**. This word means an animal without a backbone. Not all **invertebrates** are **insects** though. **Insects** have six legs and three parts to their bodies. So an ant is an **insect** but worms, snails and spiders are not.

Snail

Spider

Try This!

If you don't know the name of the bugs you've found, you can ask a grown-up or look it up in books about insects. You can find out lots of fascinating facts about these creatures.

Worm

Quick Warning!

Take a grown-up with you on a bug hunt. (They can carry a drink or a snack for you!) Don't pick the bugs up in case they could sting or hurt you. You don't want to risk hurting them either.

Ant

Slug

Plant Power

Plants and trees need water to grow.
They take water in through their roots in the ground.
This experiment shows you how the water moves
around plants and trees. Use any food coloring
you like for this experiment, but red is really good.

1. Mix some food coloring with water in an old jam jar or beaker.

2. Put some sticks of celery, with their leaves still on, into the water.

3. Watch and note what happens to the color of the celery over the next two days.

Did You Know?

Plants that grow in very dry places, like deserts, have to be good at storing water. They have large, juicy stems and leaves. Cacti are plants that can live in places without much rain.

Ouch, don't sit on that cactus!

How It Works – Let's Take a Closer Look!

Red marks start to appear on the celery leaves after a few hours. Over the next two days more and more red appears on the leaves. Water carries food to all parts of a plant or tree. This experiment shows you how water travels from the roots of a plant all the way up to its leaves.

Quick Fact!

Some trees in the rainforest can grow as tall as a 20-story building. Think of all the water going around inside them!

Rain Catcher

Make a simple gadget to catch and measure how much rain falls. You'll need an old jar or clear plastic beaker with straight sides, a small funnel and a ruler. Use some blobs of sticky tack to fix the funnel in place and stop the wind blowing it away.

1. Put the funnel into the top of the jar or beaker to make your Rain Catcher. Place it in an outside space.

2. Check it each day at the same time. Use the ruler to measure how many centimeters of rain have fallen.

3. Empty the jar each time and put it back in the same place.

4. Note the amount of rain each time in your notebook.

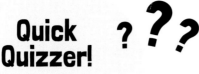

Quick Quizzer!

Do you know the name given to balls of ice that sometimes fall from the clouds?

Clue: they look like stones falling from the sky!

Don't waste the water in the Catcher. Water the plants!

Did You Know?

For some people the weather forecast is especially important. For example, farmers need to know when it will rain to decide when to plant their crops to make sure they will grow properly.

How It Works – Let's Take a Closer Look!

Rain falls when the tiny drops of water in clouds join up to make bigger ones. They get so big and heavy that they fall to the ground. The sun heats up water on the ground and turns it into **water vapor**. This rises into the air. As the **water vapor** goes higher it starts to cool down and turns back into drops of water. These make more clouds before it rains again!

Rainbow Magic

Did you know that light is a mixture of different colors? In this experiment you are going to make these different colors appear. Ask a grown-up first before using the hose in the garden. If you haven't got one, then perhaps you can find a friend who has.

1. Go out into the garden on a sunny day.

2. Point the garden hose away from you toward a dark fence or wall.

3. Stand with your back to the sun and turn the water on.

4. See what colors you can spot in the spray.

Did You Know?

When it is raining and the sun is shining at the same time you might be able to spot a rainbow. The colors of a rainbow always appear in the same order: red, orange, yellow, green, blue, indigo and violet.

Don't spray me. I don't like getting wet!

? ? ?

Quick Quizzer!

How many colors are there in a rainbow?

How It Works – Let's Take a Closer Look!

Light looks white but really it is made of many colors. When the sun shines through the water spray, the water splits the light into all these colors, and we see a rainbow. If you could mix them back together again this would make white light.

The Sky at Night

You are going to be an astronomer in this experiment. Astronomers are scientists who study the stars. Choose a clear night when the sky is not cloudy. Go out into the dark and look up into the night sky. You will see more if you can get away from street and house lights. Make sure you take a grown-up with you.

1. Take a notebook, pencil and a small flashlight into the garden or park.

2. Find somewhere to sit down and look up into the sky.

3. Write down and draw what you see. If you see patterns in the stars, then draw them.

Outdoors

26

The Big Dipper

The Southern Cross

Did You Know?

Different patterns of stars have been given names by **astronomers**. The patterns are called **constellations**. You might be able to spot The Big Dipper if you live in the northern half of the world. In the southern half, look out for the Southern Cross.

Don't mistake an airplane for a star. Airplanes have green and red lights on them.

How It Works – Let's Take a Closer Look!

Quick Quizzer

? ??

What do we call the force that keeps the Moon going around the Earth instead of just floating off?

Clue: it stops us from floating off the Earth too.

The Moon is big and easy to spot. It **orbits**, or goes round, our Earth once every 28 days and you will see different parts of it as it moves round. On a clear night you will also see thousands of stars twinkling in the sky. Stars are huge balls of very hot **gases** sending out heat and light.

Outdoors

Gravity Jump

Have you ever wondered why you don't just float off into the air when you go outside? In this experiment you are going to find out about the special force that keeps us all on the ground.

1. Go out into the garden or to the park.

2. Take some friends, and a grown-up, with you.

3. Ask your friends to jump the highest they can into the air.

4. Maybe ask the grown-up too!

When you jump into the air, all the muscles in your body have to work hard to push you up. They have to work hard because there is an invisible force called **gravity** that is pulling you toward the ground. The stronger your muscles are, the higher you will be able to jump—but you will always come back to Earth!

Did You Know?

To get into space, a rocket needs very powerful engines to push against the Earth's gravity. It needs to go about ten times faster than a bullet! In space, away from the Earth's gravity, astronauts have to have their food and drink in special packs to stop it from floating away.

Quick Fact

It is gravity that makes things fall down to the ground when we drop them.

Be a Kitchen Scientist

This part of the book is all about the science just waiting to be discovered in your kitchen. You should be able to find all of the equipment and ingredients you need for the following experiments in the kitchen already, but don't forget to ask a grown-up first before using it. Then read through the experiment before you start to check you have everything ready.

BE SAFE!

Keep a notebook handy so you can draw or write up what happens like a real scientist. You can make up your own experiments too.

Never play with heat or cleaning chemicals and always clean up afterwards!

Words to Know
Special science words are explained on page 48.

Quick Quizzer!

Answers are on page 48.

? ? ?

The Big Fizz

Stand by for some bubbling fun with this experiment. You need to stand the glass in a shallow dish or the sink to catch any overflowing froth. Don't put your face too near the glass as the fizz is very stinky!

1. Put one tablespoon of baking powder in a large glass.

2. Stand the glass inside a dish.

3. Put two tablespoons of vinegar into a small jug.

4. Pour the vinegar into the baking powder.

The baking powder and the vinegar are different types of chemicals. When they are mixed, something called a **chemical reaction** happens. The reaction makes a **gas** called **carbon dioxide** that causes all the bubbling and fizzing.

Wash everything down the sink afterwards.

Try This!

Use a funnel to put some baking powder inside a balloon. Put some vinegar in a small bottle and carefully put the balloon over the neck. Watch the balloon blow up as the powder and vinegar react.

Quick Warning!

Make sure you don't get the vinegar near your eyes or it will sting.

Kitchen

Oily Stuff

Oil and water do not mix. If you try to mix oil with water you will see that when you stop stirring, the oil stays on the top, or surface, of the water. But if you add some dish soap to the water something very interesting happens.

1. Pour some water into a bowl.

2. Add some cooking oil.

3. Now add some drops of dish soap and stir the water.

When was the last time you did the dishes?

Did You Know?

Birds have a type of oil smeared on their feathers. It keeps them waterproof so that they don't get soaking wet in the rain or on a pond.

Quick Fact!

Oil from oil tankers sometimes spills into the seas and oceans. This oil is very bad for sea birds. It floats on the top of the water and can kill them and other sea creatures.

How It Works – Let's Take a Closer Look!

The drops of oil **float** on top of the water. They have a kind of stretchy skin around them and they like to stick together. The dish soap breaks up the skin and helps to mix the oil and water together.

Get those greasy dishes clean with some dish soap!

Kitchen

35

Air Power

Trick your friends with this experiment.
No one will believe that it will work!
All you need is the kitchen sink, a plastic beaker,
some paper towel and the air around you.

1. Push the paper towel firmly into the bottom of the beaker.

2. Fill the sink with water.

3. Turn the beaker upside down. Hold it straight and push it down into the water.

4. Count to ten. Lift the beaker straight out without tipping it.

Kitchen

Quick Quizzer!

What is the name of the gas our bodies need to breathe?

Clue: you'll find its name on this page.

Did You Know?

The air around us is a mixture of gases. The main ones are called **nitrogen** and **oxygen**. Most gases are invisible but they take up space just like the air in your beaker.

How It Works – Let's Take a Closer Look!

Amazingly the paper towel does not get wet. No water gets into the beaker because the beaker is already full of air. You cannot see it but it is taking up space inside the beaker so that the water cannot get in.

Quick Fact

Some gases are very smelly. One, called hydrogen sulfide, smells of bad eggs!

Moldy Matters

You'll need two slices of bread and two chunks of cheese for this experiment, but you won't be making sandwiches with it. We're going to find out why some food needs to be kept cool.

1. Seal each slice of bread and each chunk of cheese in four separate plastic bags.

2. Put a bag of bread and a bag of cheese in the fridge. Put the other two on the windowsill.

3. Check them each day and draw or keep a note of what happens to the bread and cheese.

Did You Know?

Food stored in a freezer can keep for several months. Put a piece of cheese and a piece of bread in the freezer and you will be able to eat a cheese sandwich when you are hungry in a few months!

Keeping food fresh means less food is wasted.

Quick Warning! ⊘

Never put plastic bags near your face. Throw away the moldy bagfuls.

How It Works – Let's Take a Closer Look!

The bread and cheese on the windowsill start growing blue-green **mold** after a few days. **Mold** grows on things that are no longer fresh. Food does not go off so quickly in very cold places, like the fridge. **Mold** does not like the cold.

Quick Quizzer!

In hot weather do you think the bread and cheese will get moldy more or less quickly?

? ? ?

Be a Bedroom Scientist

This last part of the book shows you some experiments you can try out in your bedroom. As with all the other experiments, you won't need any special equipment. You should be able to find what you need in your home already, but don't forget to ask a grown-up before using them and, as usual, read through the whole experiment before you start so you know you have everything you need.

🚫 BE SAFE!

Never play with the electrical sockets and plugs in your bedroom.

Clean up your bedroom after you've finished!

Bedroom

Words to Know
Special science words are explained on page 48.

Keep a notebook handy so you can draw or write up what happens like a real scientist. You can make up your own experiments too.

CCCCC

Shadow Fun

This experiment is best done at night when it's really dark.
Close the curtains and get ready to make some weird shapes.
You can make up your own scary or funny ones too.

1. Cut a scary shape out of card.

2. Hold it in front of you, with a plain wall behind it.

3. Shine a flashlight or lamp on the card.

Bedroom

42

The holes in the card let the light of the flashlight or lamp through, but the card itself blocks the light. You get a **shadow** on the wall in the shape of the card. A **shadow** is made because the light cannot get through the card.

Quick Fact

In Indonesia they use shadow puppets to put on fantastic shows.

Try This!

Try putting your hands together as shown to make a horse's head shadow appear on the wall! Put your hands between the lamp and the wall.

See what happens when you move the shape nearer and further from the lamp.

Electric Tricks

We use lots of electricity in our homes to work everything from lights to computers. This kind of electricity moves along wires inside our houses. But there's also another type of electricity that we can make ourselves.

1. Tear a tissue into small pieces.

2. Find a plastic comb.

3. Comb your clean, dry hair about 20 times.

4. Hold the comb close to the bits of tissue.

Bedroom

44

How It Works – Let's Take a Closer Look!

When you run the comb through your hair over and over again this makes **static electricity** build up in the comb. This **static electricity** pulls the tissue paper toward the comb and makes it jump—like magic!

Turn the lights off when you leave your bedroom.

Don't waste electricity!

Quick Warning!

Never play with the electrical sockets or wires in your house.

Did You Know?

Static electricity builds up in clouds during a thunderstorm. It gets so powerful that it jumps to other clouds or to the ground in the form of a huge spark, or lightning.

Mad Mirrors

When you look in a mirror, you do not always see what you expect to see. This is very useful for tricks! Use a bit of sticky tack to keep the mirror steady.

1. Stand a small mirror upright.

2. Ask a friend to write their name on a piece of paper.

3. Put the paper in front of the mirror.

Jacob

Quick Fact

Mirrors break easily because many are made of glass.

Your friend's name looks back-to-front in the mirror! **Reflections** are always the wrong way around like this. If you wave at yourself in a mirror with your right hand, it will look as if you are waving your left. It is called a **mirror image**.

Try This!

Find a full-length mirror on a wardrobe or wall. Stand very close to the edge of it. Lift one arm and one leg.

If you haven't got a full-length mirror at home, try this in a clothes shop!

Words to Know

Air pressure – The force that air places on everything it touches.

Astronomer – A scientist who studies the stars and everything in space.

Carbon dioxide – It is the gas that is put into fizzy drinks to make the fizz. It is also the gas our bodies breathe out into the air.

Chemical reaction – This is when two or more chemicals are mixed together and they change and make something new.

Condensation – When a gas changes into a liquid. Water vapor, or steam, changes into drops of water when it touches something cold.

Constellations – These are patterns of stars in the sky. Astronomers give them names.

Elastic – Something which can return to its normal shape after being stretched.

Float – To stay on the top, or surface, of liquid.

Gas – The air around us is a mixture of different gases, like oxygen and nitrogen. A gas does not have a shape of its own.

Gravity – A force that pulls things toward the Earth.

Insect – An invertebrate with six legs and three parts to its body.

Invertebrate – A creature without a backbone.

Liquid – Water is a liquid. Liquids can be poured and do not have a shape of their own.

Mirror image – This is the way your reflection looks in the mirror. It is the wrong way round to the real you!

Mold – A very small type of fungus. It grows on things that are going bad.

Nitrogen – A gas which makes up a large part of the air around us.

Nutrients – The foodstuff that plants or animals need to grow well. Plants get nutrients from the soil.

Orbit – The path of something that is travelling around a star or planet. The Earth orbits the Sun. The Moon orbits the Earth.

Oxygen – A gas in the air around us, which our bodies need to be able to breathe.

Reflection – You see a reflection when light rays bounce off you and on to a mirror. The light rays bounce back from the mirror and into your eyes.

Refraction – When light changes direction as it goes into water. This makes you see objects in water in a different way.

Shadow – A shadow is made when light cannot go through something to reach the other side.

Solid – Solid things, like bars of soap and toothbrushes, have a shape of their own.

Static electricity – This is a kind of electricity that does not move. It is not like the electricity we use for lights and other gadgets.

Surface – The top of something. The surface of water is where it meets the air.

Water vapor – The gas that comes off hot or warm water. It is also called steam.

Quick Quizzer Answers

Page 5 – steam

Page 7 – shampoo

Page 9 – it will sink

Page 13 – no, it will look straight

Page 17 – a bird

Page 19 – a spider

Page 23 – hail

Page 25 – seven

Page 27 – gravity

Page 37 – oxygen

Page 39 – if it isn't in the fridge, it will get moldy more quickly